C.J. Caj was born in Winthrop, Massachusetts. He grew up with his five older sisters and a single working mother, a nurse, living in poverty. He was trained and worked as a chef in both Boston and Munich, Germany. Caj is recovering from both alcohol and drug addiction. This is the world through his eyes.

For all of the people

I've taken to hell

I hope you can get a ride back.

C.J. Caj

POEMS FROM THE THIRD RAIL

AUSTIN MACAULEY PUBLISHERS™

LONDON • CAMBRIDGE • NEW YORK • SHARJAH

Ordering Information
Quantity sales: Special discounts are available on quantity purchases by corporations, associations, and others. For details, contact the publisher at the address below.

Publisher's Cataloging-in-Publication data
Caj, C.J.
Poems from the Third Rail

ISBN 9781638292401 (Paperback)
ISBN 9781638292425 (ePub e-book)

Library of Congress Control Number: 2023908154

www.austinmacauley.com/us

First Published 2023
Austin Macauley Publishers LLC
40 Wall Street, 33rd Floor, Suite 3302
New York, NY 10005
USA

mail-usa@austinmacauley.com
+1 (646) 5125767

To my sister Meg, who never left me in my years of darkness.

You let me into your heart, and you kept me there, I love you Margaret.

For my kids Jeremy and Josephine and their mother Jessica.

The amount of grace, compassion, forgiveness and love you have bestowed upon me in my life, even when I was sick and suffering, fills my heart with love. Your mom brought you to all those rehabs and hospitals to bring a smile and hope, those visits kept me fighting. I love all of you with all of my heart.

Thank you for your Grace

Table of Contents

For Leanna

My therapist
You are the light
Of grace
In the human form
Of compassion
Our time is sacred

You saved me

When my nerves
Were on
The third rail
I was laying down
On the tracks
When I found you

You found in me
The different ways
To make the trains
Stop from coming
Before it was too late

I am eternally grateful
For you Leanna
For being there
When I needed you

The most.

The Phoenix

With the self-infliction
Of the incendiary flames
To be the ashes
From self-immolation
Of the soul

Black searing heat
Fusing agony
To a mind
That cannot break
Until the world crumbles

Smoldering
Until your core implodes
The death of self
Surrendering of will

To be molded
With your very own hands
To be the bird
Of your imagination

Only if you are willing to die
Will you fly high
To the infinite pinnacle
Of the phoenix.

My Mind Is a Scape

Twin poles
Separated at birth
Two continents
Pulling away from each other
Until they collide
A chunk of me
Has sheared off

Bi-polar isn't just up and down
It's two octopuses
Fighting with knives
The king with the sword one day
Content with the grave the next
An invisible civil war
The victor determined
Every day

So little time in the middle
For moments like this
When the past and the present
Just became the future
When I'm up, I wanna stay up

When I am down,
All the pain comes back
Covered with insecurity

I use the pain to climb
Climbing and climbing
Always climbing
I have come to find the beauty
In the beating and the comeback
Laughing at time in the face

The maniac does all the writing
Desperate
To makes his words immortal
The lost and hopeless one
Left to start the fires
To be doused
With blood and ink

Somehow lit

With wet matches

Ten Thousand Chambers

Living is a game
It started in the womb
The guns back then were toys
They shot caps and water

As children, we had cravings
Always the desire for more and more
More love and joy and smiles
More attention and affection and play things

As our bones stretched and grew
Eyes widened and sharpened
Tender hearts and expanding minds
Cravings and desires grew

When I was young and cool and in control
Life was a game of checkers
Simple moves and easy wins
Jump-jump-jump king me

Then the board got flipped
Chess pieces dominated the field
Complex moves and serious decisions
One wrong move and the king was dead

Most of the populous can deal
Reset the pieces and move on
Addicts get trapped in the battle
Stealing horses and running away
From castles with bars

In the chaos and frenzy of war
We get wounded all the time
We drink morphine and inject alcohol
Playing with loaded guns

Holding a handful of shells
In a chamber of 10,000 or more
The barrel spins with such ease
It may take a 1000 life-sparing clicks

With one flash and a bang
Just one
To settle the score forever
Boom

Game over.

A Prayer for God

Does anyone pray for you, my lord?
For you are responsible
For so many children
Watching angels
And demon-faced hell bats
Fighting for our souls

Witnessing wars and genocide
The benevolent peacekeepers
Providing security and refuge
For the innocent victims and children
Earthly evidence of you power and grace
Your purpose for our creation

You instilled a freewill
In every beating heart
You gave us a mind tied to a soul
We defy the laws of natural order
Shooting a telescope a million miles
deep into space

To catch a glimpse
To take the film
of your celestial divinity
Our beginning

May your God
Bless you, my God
May He bless your son Jesus
All the saints and the angels
Mother Mary
And your flock of souls
Safe in the kingdom of Heaven!

Amen.

I Am

The existential prototype
Of the beyond poor
Writer and humble artist

Buying paint over bacon
Always great literature on nose
Cult and film noir
Filling my gaps of conscience

Always hungry over the keys
My un-satiated mind wanders
With someone else's feet
Places that need to be found

Discovery
In the absence
Of everything
There can be no dark
Without light
Never found

The search is
The destination
The journey is now
Or forever lost

I can only see myself
Against that background
The mirror that reflects
All that is nothing
I am everything I am not
A reverse negative copy

I am born again in every poem
They are cloned parts of my soul
That I give away freely

A drug more powerful
Than my imagination's
Outer limits

A capsule bitten
Between teeth and faith
Half the antidote
Half of the poison
A pill taken every time
In sleep and wake

For nourishment and survival
To interpret the insanity
Of today's reality

I try to make
My words sweet enough
For one day
I may have to eat them
Washing them down
With old tears
And future fears
Rich or poor
Happy or not
I will be forever

Full

To Bear Witness

To the war raging in the east
Mother Russia is trying to kidnap her child back
Ukraine has been attacked by
Such as small man in stature and heart
Putin murders opponents and journalists
A communist's autocratic dream to crush democracy
A Nazi's heart in a Napoleonic body
The first of many rockets that were launched
Targeted civilian apartment buildings
Maternity wards, hospitals, and everything
For nothing
The maniacal mentality is to kill
Kill babies and children
Before they become parents and soldiers
His idol Hitler would be thrilled with his first move
Ukrainian parents are writing their children's names
On their children's backs in permanent marker
In case they get separated
Their name and date of birth
Mama's and Papa's phone number if they get lost
In the mass exodus of humanity

Tragically some never to be reunited
Praying another family raises them well
Train stations are being bombed mercilessly
As the refugees flee towards safer ground
The U.S. and NATO are arming them to the teeth
Bullets, rockets, and robots
Tank killing death drones
Soldiers with a joy stick and a trigger
Virtual battlefield warriors
Our boots on the ground could light the wick of WW3
A global powder keg balanced on the tip of a sword
Germany is chipping in
With support and a few thousand helmets
Somewhat valuing human life
Over a natural gas pipeline from the source of evil
We all need money and electricity
Right?
Did they forget what they have done?
Who they were when Dresden was burning?
The gas will flow
During and after the war
Business as usual

The world cannot afford to find out
If he alone will punch in the codes and hit the button
The dream of a megalomaniac before his death
A tactical nuclear war
The most brutal and delusional autocrat alive
He wants to carve his own Russian Mt. Rushmore
Himself besides Lenin and Stalin
And someone the terrible or the great

Too many men from one birthplace
That execute their own civilians and enemies
Killing their neighbors
Enemy or not for absolute power
Win or lose, he will erect more statues of himself
A marble and bronze facade of greatness
Only to be torn down one day
We pray for sooner than never
As mothers, children, the elderly, and sick
Are moved out of harm's way
Space is created for the brave Ukrainian patriots
To wave their blue and yellow flag
In the face of the hammer and the sickle
Willingly spilling their blood for family and country
Their soil will be stained
Never to be taken
Citizens and soldiers will fight to the death
For every heart that is stopped
Is to keep their brother's and sister's
Heart beating
Do you know the cost?
Of your life and freedom

Don't you dare ever

Take it for granted.

Cigarette Ash in My Coffee

Just enough
To add a smoky note
To my already strong
Jet-black French Roast

I'm listening to Eddie Vedder
Singing to me
All of the lullaby's
Only the heavenly soloist
And his Ukulele

I am poor in the sense
That I have no money
Nothing except
My soul possessions
Canvases and paper
Vinyl and paint
I got a roof
And just enough food

My typewriter and these ink stains
The only vessels I have
To shout my truth to the world
From every rooftop
Which I will stand
Throwing copies off

Into the wind one day

I create
Without electricity or wires
Such as the music is being played
Strings and voice in orchestra
The symphony of my heart and the keys

Perfect
Beauty
In the purest form

Of simplicity

How to Write a Good Poem

Insert paper
Into typewriter

Pause

Go back in time
Carry
The heaviest
Suitcase
You can find
Open said suitcase
Take out anything

Blunt or sharp
Try both
Open a wound
Bleed deeply
Wring out your stain
Type and strike
Your dark blood
Into pulp
Leaving evidence

Of your pain
On paper
Till long after

You are dust.

I Slipped

Into the dark character
That is my own ghost
She wrapped her cloak
Around every cell
Of my being
That has ever sinned
Protecting every muscle
Of my heart that has been torn
And gauged with thorns
My heart only beating
The next breath
Weeping
Dark pink tears
Of pain and surrender
Wishing
There was no tomorrow
Yet, it arrives every day
On time

The Devil and his children
Are at recess
In the most dangerous part

Of me
Toying in my conscience
Cruelly playing games
Of illusions
Teasing me of a better life
In the beyond
Daring me to play with them
And follow them home
I hide and never I seek
I pick myself second
To die
And the last to live
Because
I want to live
I never want to make
A final decision

That is permanent and forever

Please don't ever you

Shot Glass Lenses

My shift is over a 1 AM
My Irish bar oasis Whitey's
The best dive in South Boston
Just a green door and no sign
The sweetest stench
Of the sticky floors
Stale beer and bitter dreams
My stool stinks of the regulars
Danny the bartender and owner
Former boxer and the only bouncer
Bourbon on the rocks and a draft waiting
As always

With a nod my tab starts running
Always the same souls
Always the same problems and gripes
The weather and the Red Sox suck
My job sucks and my back hurts

Our haven to forget and escape it all
Through my six-shot glass lenses
The city looks rosy
My miserable life is microscopic

My wife's knees will be still locked
When I stagger home

The carpenter and the mailman
An off-duty cop and the bum
The old man that never talks and mumbles
Into the mirror
Until last call after hours

And me the late-night chef

At the end of the bar
Sits the middle-aged hag
She buys her own gin and tonics
She has something pretty
Left behind the pain
Lonelier than I am
She rents a room above the bar
A convenient walk up the backstairs
When my wife asked where I was
I told her

"I slept in my car"

The Maker and the Mold

Have I not become?
The creator unto self?
After the clay dust
Was clapped off of
God's very own hands
As the Devils and Spirits
Were cast
Out of the light of shadow
That soon becomes death
For the living

Self-awareness
The mental and fatal flaw
Of all mankind
Inflicted upon our creation
Such poor and blind
Creatures we are
Feverishly searching
Through an un-winnable maze
Reaching high
For dead end cliffs
And the hopes to fly

The American dream
Was just that
Only a dream

Malleable mental sheep
Wrapping light years
Of internet optics
Around their psyches
And throats

Thew Web suffocates and
Synthesizes our voices

All for lack of truth
And confidence
We condemn and obey
The collective
Of artificial intelligence
The creator of desires
Material and emotional
And a full-filler of none

When I am done
When my creator
The maker of me
Calls on me
To leave this realm
Shall my hands and bones
Be bruised and broken
To make my mold

Unbreakable
In the light

Towards heaven.

Black Dog

His howls and whimpers
The first echoes
To reverberate
Into my conscience
His large and looming presence
Obscured and hidden
Following in my shadow

I was always attracted
Towards
His vicious bark
Desperate not to be alone
I chased and stumbled
Until I fell into his
Magnetic trap

The ultra-depressive center
Stole the air
From my lungs
Choked the word help
From my throat
I had to choose

The rope or the bottle
I drained
Hundreds of bourbon barrels
To use as rafts
Sticky whisky residue
clouded my brain
Pulling me out
Too far under

I tried to drink
A German brewery dry
Suspended in a foam capped
Amber ocean
Drowning was impossible
The spirits

Kept me alive.

Enabled

I let everyone
Do everything for me
It was my first addiction
My first affliction
My first disabling flaw

I'm just shaking the habit
Now

Ma let me nip
From her dusty bottles
Cordials and coffee brandy
It was easier for her to ignore

Than to care or listen

My sisters saw
That I was broken and sad
They supplied the beer and pot
The only medicine
They had

To help save their little brother

They gave me harder drugs
When the light stuff
Stopped working
That's what they used for pain
We were all in the same canoe

Just our hands to paddle
In circles

When it came to partner
And wife
We both needed
To settle
I needed security

She wanted kids

As long as I paid the bills
She wouldn't look
My way
I thought I was sneaky
And clever

Drinking behind the bedroom door

All of the people in my life
Got used like old crutches
Tossed aside
When they could help no more

Cutting ties
Was their toughest love

Dejected
Helpless and angry
I kept going to the well
Until the bucket was gone
Not a sip of a puddle

At the bottom

I was alone

with my echo.

Milk Carton

Stuck on top of the Ferris wheel
Tall enough standing on my toes
On the top of the world
Breathlessly swinging and gasping

My sister punched my leg to stop
"You'll slip and die."
With my devilish grin
A few more rocks for fun

The scary rides thrilled me
My eyes as big as the flashing bulbs
Never fearing being spun like a top
Tossed and crushed and whipped around

Biting down on the last crunch
Of a red candy apple
I begged my sisters
For cotton candy

I got to reach high
And pay the $2 myself
A double-fisted sugar overload
Chomping at the blue and pink cloud

I wandered toward the games
Went to my favorite games
The air-powered army rifles
Shooting a 100 BBs at the red paper star

Water balloons popping on clowns heads
Plastic rings skipping off of glass bottles
Darts popping little balloons like firecrackers
The sound was a symphony to my childish ears

I came back from space
I startled awake
The symphony crashed
Guns fired faster
Peppering the dented metal
Louder, louder—too loud
The balloons wouldn't stop popping
My eyes burst like the water balloon

Tears poured like thunder
My cheeks were on fire
With hot pins and needles
The summer air escaped me
Five older sisters and they all vanished

I started to run nowhere
Anywhere they were
My sneakers slipping on the gravel and dirt
Snot and ride tickets fell to the ground
A thousand directions to go in

No familiar heads on the bumper cars
No pretty faces holding stuffed prizes
The whipping Round-Up too blurry to see
And they wouldn't go on the Ferris wheel without me

I knew they love fried dough
Right back where we started
No sisters with powdered faces
No cinnamon dusted noses to be seen

I closed my eyes and screamed
In a blink the carnival was spinning
Around like a merry-go-round horse race
The polarity of my mind
Was a roller coaster in reverse
In an empty car alone
They were gone

Three hands grabbed my shoulders
All my nightmares were confirmed
I'was getting snatched
I was never going home again

Worried and happy smiles looked down
"Oh sweetie, there you are."
They handed me
A big bouquet of colored balloons
And an Incredible Hulk poster
I let the balloons fly into the night
I dropped the poster
And crushed it under my knees

I hugged all their legs
Locking us together

I wanted to hold on forever.

Sirens

I woke up
Dead again
I laid still
The nightmare
Still playing

I waited for
The sirens to wail
I expected
The flashing lights
To penetrate

I was desperate
And begging
For mercy and escape
From hell

I was silent
The dream
Was muted
I prayed to God
At bedtime

For my ghost
To take me
To the closet
To hang me
With my favorite necktie

Navy blue
With yellow hornets

No sirens
No lights

I woke up
Just
Dead again.

An Addicts Last Prayer

Oh, dear God
We can't follow your signs
Or find your path
Taking only wrong turns
Making the gravest of mistakes
There are no maps in our heart
No compass we can point
Each moment is a fight
The struggle is surreal
Every morning that we rise
Expecting great light
The darkness consumes
We can't escape last night
Insanity grows wild
Our minds are infected
The rope is getting tighter
Our will to live
Is slipping away
Our parents are weeping
While we are abusing

Our babies are sleeping
Our spouses
Can't sleep a wink

There must be a way
For freedom one day
In the grips of evil
We are all
Good sick people
Please God
Find in us
What we need
What we have lost
Faith and trust
In you
We will put down the bottle
Throw away the needle
Just for this day
We can stay away

Addiction
Is our evil curse.

Pills

One sad
One crazy
Twice a day
With water and food
To stabilize insanity
To save me from drowning
In the ocean intentionally
Or cracking your skull
Wide open
For balance on sunbeams
To navigate mania and madness
Not to cry
Watermelon-sized tears
Into my pillow
Or smash
A passage through
The liquor store window

Pills are
Chemical spellcheck
For encrypted feelings
When only curses

Are formed
Kill is the only switch
Always on
Never off
I thank science
For Lithium
And these two tiny pills

A Block of Writing

Inside the verses
Are crystalized
Black coal diamonds
The sharpest facets cut
Waiting to capture
The words in pain

And the few seeds that blossom

It's an acrid perfume
That draws me in
To the rocky bottomless shore
A shipwreck
Of my own navigation

I flow with the cold and hot currents

A magnetic destination toward a song
That holds me captive and waiting
I see through a sun-drenched mirror

Reflecting all of the faces
Of humanity and hell
I pause to look for the heavens

I search deep for self
In the land
Of the dead and the living
Drinking my salty tears
Praying they be turned into water

The faintest echoes
Of laughter and joy
Bouncing around the ethos
Inside of my brain
Black nights and blue days

I am as still
As the universe spins around me
When I write again
I will stand on a wave
And gently reach for the stars

Adjusting the light

For this singularity of thought

Of this

Mindful moment.

Coffee Stains

Ugly
Oh, so ugly
In the morning
More ghastly
At night
I am handsome
Behind the frown
And under the wrinkles
My face is splintered
With red crow's feet
It must be the bulbs
These damn bulbs
Perhaps candles
Will shed
A more flattering light
What happened?
The decades run fast
My sneakers
Are dirty and slow
If I quit cigarettes

Then maybe
I can chase
More air in my lungs

Less gasp
In my breath
My teeth
Are brown and straight
They used to be
Crooked and white
I pull my skin firm
Pinch the cracks
Smooth
Left eye closed
Right eye squinting

Now that that looks like
An old photo of me

Chinatown Boston 2022

Every day, this August
Is cremating the heat record
The tropics have arrived
The city is on fire

My last $200 bucks
Jumping out of my pockets
To be blown
On every Asian pleasure

Twenty smokes and 20 nips
To prime the pump
It's been two years
Since I got proper drunk

Drinking and watching Chinese chess
With my fat pumpkin toothed friend Sam
An old and proud Chinese soldier
That killed the rebels in delight

Lunch of Sapporo and Peking Duck
Dim Sum and a blond lady
She ordered too much food
We joined tables for a feast

Great conversation
Very little attraction
She wanted me, I wanted less
It made me a little horny

Last oasis of the day
Long cold stairwell up
For a much needed massage
The 'Coup de Gras' of a perfect day

I was too drunk
For the happy ending
I tipped her $20 anyway
So she didn't feel like
A prostitute

For an hour.

Fucked up and Sad

I'm still very drunk
Every muscle in my body relaxed
My mini hedonistic vacation in Chinatown
Has done me very well.

At Quincy Center
Waiting for the train
To take me to the bus home
Smoking alone on the last bench

Catching the artificial breeze
From the opposite train
Headed Downtown
Up popped a kid and sat right down
Shaking sweat over a tourniquet and needle

He asked me for something shiny or a phone
Then asked me to shoot him up in his neck
All the tracks down to his toes were collapsed
W steady hands of a chef
I confirmed it was Fentanyl and agreed

I was dripping with curious excitement
I had never seen this before up close
I thought twice
He thought once without thinking

Pointed at a faint blue line
Took a stab without faith
He drained the needle into his forearm
I asked how long for affect

Four...three...two
His heads bounced into a vertical pillow
That is the Subway Map
Needled dropped, bag in the wind
Slumped and nodded
He died but for how long

The summer thunder
Cracked the rain
The train came and I pulled away
Looking down, I was thinking

I will deal with the Devil
In my own hand
A bottle to be picked up
Or thrown down

Heroin is like real sugar
It's good for you now
Fentanyl
The medicine to kill elephants

Available cheap for the masses
Obliteration of a sub culture
There's no coming back from that

Now that's

Really fucked up

And sad.

Kicked

Straight in the balls
I can taste them
In my throat
Reality checked
All the boxes

The most impossible
Mind-numbing
Thought
To never drink
Again

No ice-cold beer
On the beach
While eating fried clams
By the
Seaside shack

No red wine
At the bistro in Paris
Watching
Sophisticated women

Passing with elegance
No sips
Of sweet bubbles
After my daughter
Has taken
Her vows

No bitter whiskey
As I take shots
Playing pool
Missing the board
Throwing darts

The nights of Manhattans
And Martinis
To calm my nerves on a first date
Making her much more
Attractive than she really was

All of this is gone now
Washed away
In the flood
With my cars and homes
My family and my friends

Absolute truth
Be told
This sucks.
Sober
Means sober.

My First Girl Gone

She was there
To pour liquid
On my very first wound

Her magic elixir
Instant relief from agony
Suffered from birth

Back then
No visible scars were left
Like I say she was magic

With insecure thoughts
At the eighth-grade dance
When my shoulders were tight

My juvenile nerves trembled
She massaged my neck
For relief

I was cocky with courage
I got a dance with the pretty
Catholic school girl

A goodnight kiss
After
The last slow dance

When the high-pressure
Chef jobs
Made me frantic and insane

It was she who tucked me into bed
A reprieve
From the long day's chaos

I was told I was with her
Too often
That she was making me sick

I told everyone
To leave us alone
How dare they?

They didn't understand
Our love
We needed each other

We drank
From
Each other's overflowing cup

She was right by my side
When my marriage
And career were over

There were more cries and pleas
For me to leave her
We grew closer than ever before

I couldn't survive without her
She was my heartbeat
And breath

A companion
That never rejected
Our love was like no other

They said
She was my weakness
I say strength

When I crashed the trucks and cars
She was my lone passenger
Before and after each calamity

We were inseparable
Until the law stepped in
At the risk of imprisonment

I was forced to abandon her
Immediate separation
No hug or kiss goodbye

The judge ruled rehab over prison
If I could have taken her with me
I would have
Chose prison every time

Six months left
In a two-year stint
I write about her every day

Each moment
In my thoughts
When our lips touch again

I will drink her in slowly
Let her wash down my throat
Feel her lust warming my core

Easing my nerves
Erasing my worries
Soothing my soul

The sweetest

Drunken kiss.

Sunday Morning

The sky is light black
I am dreaming
Of a feathered chorus
The birds wrestle me
Awake

Those hungry and chirping
Sons of bitches
I want to shoot them
Clear off the wire
Choke their tiny little necks
Wipe out their species
Beyond extinction

For Christ's sake

It's Sunday morning.

Cigarettes and Booze

And many decisions
A small price tag
Just a bit short

Little under a million

I coulda bought boats
and fancy cars
I settled

For crushed cans
And ashes

Coulda built a mansion
Or traveled the world
Had many women

Diamonds for them all

My wallet is scorched
All the plastic has melted

I am disappearing
From the family photo

Looking back
They were all

Bad decisions.

Jesus Christ!

Your father sent you
To deliver the gospels
The Bible's thematic tone
Sinner and nonbelievers
Be damned into hell
Forever

JESUS CHRIST!
That is a harsh punishment
We are mortal and full of sin
You sacrificed your self
To absolve of such sin
That was the deal…right?

JESUS CHRIST!
The priests that came to your calling
Raped altar boys and innocent children
The pope in his Vatican castle
Covered for them all
Did you do any interviews?
Ask for references?

JESUS CHRIST!
When a child is taken to heaven
Christian parent suffer in faith
"God needs them in His kingdom"
"Amongst his flock"

Why? May I ask is that?

JESUS CHRIST!
Waves of holy crusaders
Slaughtered in your name
Vicious punishment
For having no faith in you
Was that in the fine print?

JESUS CHRIST!
The Jews rejected your Father's offering
They were waiting for a different Christ
The believed the first half of the story
Six million souls starved and cremated
Is there any reason why?
You let that happen?
You were a Jew !

JESUS CHRIST!
Can we be saved?
Did we do something wrong?
Or is it too late?
Will you be revealed?
Under tomb and grave

In your proper name
The Christ Jesus
I ask of your father
To please send us a daughter
A natural protector
With a mother's

Loving heart

The Virus

It came from the east
Alarm bells rang
America turned a deaf ear
Then everything

Stopped

The invisible killer
Is everywhere
It ravages the sick
Extinguishes the elderly

That's bad

Most children

Are spared
From its tangles

That's good

Schools are shuttered

Yellow buses abandoned
And left hollow
Classrooms on virtual computers
The kids are finally plugged in
That was always the plan

Right?

No more school massacres
That's good
The school bully
Has to stay at home
That's good

No jobs anywhere
That's bad
Everyone
Is in big brother's pocket
That's bad
His Uncle Sam
Is footing the food bill
That's good

The self-proclaimed
President king
Trump's gold over lives
The coldest calculation
That's bad
"The killer is a hoax"
He shouts
With ferocious pomp

And zero stature
A slithering serpent reigns
He tells his cult followers
To drink bleach
They blindly follow
Perishing into ashes
Urns and early graves
That's very bad

The Left

Proud blue
Union backed
The working class Joe

They let bad teachers
Keep teaching bad

They want no borders
"Let them all in,"
"Illegal or otherwise."

"Melt into the bottom of our pot"
To shake their pockets

We can't
Take care of our own
Population

Elderly living
In poverty, choosing
Between food or medicine

Where is the money
Going to come from?

Trees?
Grow more trees?
Hug a tree?

Is that your solution?

The Middle

(Class)

The Right

White
Hard right
In full control
Conservation
Of conservative power
It's a cult now
With their own militias

They didn't only drum
To their own beat
They killed
The orchestra
Sending the Left crowd
Screaming

They let the elephant loose
In the theater
So many people got trampled
They only see red
Blood-red
Their new leader
Jumped

From the T.V. screen

The self-proclaimed
President king
Has the power
All the power
Of hate and malice
White power
Reigns supreme

"This is our country."
"Get off our land."

Is there no taking it back?

January 6th

Wow!
What a fucked up day!
The plan of a bloody Coup'
Came into play for real
On the president's last day
He called for
The vice president's head
Cut off or hung from the gallows
Outside on the capitol's lawn
That his armed loyalists built

To be used that day
No way erected as symbol

In this country of freedom
Based deep in democracy
The whitest of hate
Was on full display
For the world to see
Half our country agrees
That he should have succeeded
All because

They believed
Their votes were stolen
And didn't count

Now that's

A scary

And fucked up day.

Desperation

Not a good look
On anyone
It hangs off of you
Like a cheap, pathetic suit

A tattered dress
Veiled in self-double
Wrapped in
Fragile insecurity

Settling for anything
Anything is more than nothing
Nothing is never enough
It never has been

I am a shape-shifter
Without a shape of my own
A social chameleon
With a 1000 personalities

A cunning and convincing actor
A disposable mask

For whatever I need
A material and emotional vampire

To fill what my empty shell
Was desperate for
An unquenchable craving for attention
Good or bad, I craved it

Squeezing out love
Where there was none
Awkward and overbearing
Displays of affection
The desired attention
Never reciprocated
Misinterpreted as failure
And stinging rejection

Who do I want?
Who do I want to be?
What is missing?
That I can't find?
I have only my self
To offer the world
My truth in pain and joy

If you stay

I will show you the shadow

Behind the mask.

Faith Alarm

All the sirens are wailing
I am yelling and crying
My nerves
Are being ripped out
My heart
Just fell from my chest
It was to be another
Innocent text from my ex
A simple hello
The kids
Are doing well
Everything is OK
Horrible words
Burned across the screen
My eyes repelled
With disbelief
My childhood brother friend
Died the night before
Nine years
Minus one day
My other brother friend
Died the same way

Demons and addiction
Defeated them both
How could my newly found God?
Need them in His kingdom
Let Heaven's angels
Lift them up
They were only young
And suffering
They are children
Of God
Uncles and sons
Fathers and brothers
Friends to so many
I want to drink pills
And eat whiskey
Numb and escape
Chase the same demons
They did
The Devil's net
Won't catch me
I sit here now
Aching and praying
Breathing and typing
Searching
For an answer
That God will reveal
When I die
In His time
Certainly
Not mine

Dark Corner

My mind is midnight black
In that distant intersection
Resides my private theater
Where the horror shows play

I only go there with a candle
Never a flashlight or a torch
To drop off film and escape
Weld shut the wide doors
Behind me

I am the villain
And the monster
I know the plots by heart
Created in my daydreams
And nocturnal hallucinations

I twist my head
Over both shoulders
I creep away slowly
A character on the screen
May have jumped and followed

With a knife in teeth
And mask over face
I dash back to my place
Not to be caught
By myself or the past

If you dare
Watch
I will pirate you a scene
You must view it in private
No children under 17

When you are done screaming
I must burn the film
If you stole the evidence
Another crime
I will have commit

It was all in self-defense
Humanity
Made me do it.

Charred

Burned
With pride
No match needed
For destruction

Gone with a strike
Of lightening
Thunder crumbling
All the roads behind

No paths out
Road signs
Are buried
Deep in the mud

Bridges
In every direction
Left torched
And charred

A charcoal wire
To be walked alone
With nothing but arms
For balance

Was being right?

Worth it?

Fuck

One beer makes my thirsty
Eighteen beers and an empty box
Takes me back to the liquor store

Bourbon this time
And a pack of smokes
More buzz and a stronger punch

One beer I break out in cuffs
One pint of liquor
I'm sleeping on a metal cot
Only my hands for a pillow

One beer
On my breath
I can't see me kids
I have lost their trust again

One beer
I crash another car
I haven't killed anyone
Yet

One beer
Takes away my freedom
Locks me in my bedroom
Alone with a bottle of booze

FUCK

I'm thirsty
I only want one

Docket # 666

Jim Beam v/s me
Date: Last night

A mountain of evidence
Open and shut case
A walk-over for the prosecution
Held until trial

Shackled on the stand
Swearing at the Bible
Truth promised to God
With my fingers crossed

I'm going to hell and solitary

No exculpatory evidence
To get me off the hook
The judge cracks the gavel
I could get life in a bar

Or worse
The quick death sentence
Do I want to hang?
Or face the firing squad
Tough decision

I'll take the bullet
At least
I get a blindfold
And one last cigarette

My final meal request

A bottle of bourbon and
A chaser.

Bukowski

Raw
Unfiltered
Filthy
Genuine
Genius
Obscene
Desperate
Depraved
Disgusting
Perverted
Found
Lost
Confused
Drunk
Transparent
Tar-stained
Wounded
Repulsive
Tortured
Loved
Despised
He taught me to read

He taught me about
Hate and love

Bukowski showed me
How to spill my soul
He was a dirty, old man

Just like me

Rafter

Black feather * black feather
From who's wing * have you flown?
You are my * quill in ink
I pen my pain * in poem

I was plucked of a coal bird

With your finger and thumb
You were fast and hard asleep
Heavy drunken on rum

I cannot see * this bird of prey
That you speak * that you say
Perhaps maybe *just possibly
He simply flew * far away

Dear sir * dear sir
I wish this be true
I grant to you * another guess
All without a clue
Has he hidden * did he poke?
On this paper * what I have wrote

All my words * have long forever
Been stuck * in my throat

No sir, no sir
This surely is not the case
He is right here
In this very same place

Did I kill * your bird with shock?
Stabbed him with * my evil thought
Exposed to him *a broken soul
an open wound * my broken heart *

Wrong sir * wrong sir
He surely * is alive
Where he * is standing
May be * a surprise

Tell me, feather * Tell me, friend

I must see * Where is he?

Silly sir, * silly sir
Look straight down
Both your feet are swaying
Just above the ground

This black bird * that you stalk and seek
Is pecking fast * with its beak
Is perched above * on your noose
To set you free * to cut you loose

Hurry sir, * hurry sir
To save yourself * take feather in hand
With ink and paper * you shall mend
This book's chapter * is not your end
You must write

Till your destiny ends.

Ink Poison

The worms burrow deep
In my sludge-filled mind
Filthy and rotten
Deranged dark thoughts
I dig at the headless monsters
With my fingers and paper spades
Chisel them with keys
Poison them with dark purple ink
The creatures only grow larger
Mysteriously morphing
Into toxic snakes
Sharp coils and teeth
Serpents with a divine code
Hidden letters and messages
Encrypted literature
Translated in poem
I cannot catch them in a net
I tried to exterminate them
With strong drugs and alcohol
Too slippery to grasp
Cut one in half
Two more are formed

More heads to invade
An indestructible force
When I hear their rattle
My nerves vibrate
My fingers twitch
Pain blurs my eyes
I load blank white sheets
Type, type, type the madness
It's a powerful drug
I love this drug
Smoking cigarettes
Sucking on 26 letters
Spitting the truth
Never biting my tongue
Such a bitter and sweet taste
That never satiates
Sour kisses
Keep the monsters happy
We are symbiotic
We need each other
We devour each other
We are each other
Until we both die.

I Am

The thief
When you lock
Me out

I am
The wound
You dig your nails into

I am
Your nightmare
When you feel safe

I am
Your scream
When I steal your voice

I am
The song
That bleeds your ears

I am
The man
Who stands on your heart

You are
The only one
Who broke me

Twice.

Whore

Do whores?
Know they are whores?
Are they proud of the fact
That men prefer whores
On the first date
Expecting
Virgin-like obedience
Thereafter
Whores need practice
To master their craft
With vocal and sexual gymnastics
Blowing minds
And so much more
Men come to despise
The whore
She is the whore of all whores
For being a whore
Someone else's whore
When she isn't your whore
Anymore.

Train Goddess

My journey home on the rails
Thank God for them
They bring me to my women!
I just fucked Michelle
She was crashed on pills
That's when she lets me
Fuck her in the ass
Morning sex
Always makes me happy
Halfway back home now
Government Center station is eerily empty
Not one soul to be seen
Boston in the summer
Very strange
The virus stopped everything
I am all alone
Dancing wildly to L.A Woman
The Doors groove
Through parts of my soul
Next trolley to the train connection
Coming in five minutes
The bulbs flicker and glow

The fans swirl sticky air
The city is desolate
The city is mine
Calm and peaceful
I'm still standing alone
The music faded
Sweet cherry pheromones fill the air
Ascending from the lower platform
Is an angel
An earthly goddess
A tangible gift from the heavens
What a beautiful creature
He has created!
She strides past

I inhale the essence
Of her morning shower
Coconut and flowers
Her black shiny hair bouncing
And caressing her shoulders
A scant tan line
The outline
Of her modest bathing suit
Peeking out at me
She's a good girl
I'm getting hard
Her mask obscures her face
What perfect lips she must have
Soft and wet and red

I see her soul
In her dark crystal eyes
Manicured eyebrows
Aquiline Roman nose
She is perfect
I slow my dance
To a more gentle rhythm
One I know she will like
One she will feel
I'm sending out my vibes
They are strong
Trying to be on her radar
The platform fills in
Blurry figures mingle
The strangers are invisible
Leaning on a pole
I can't hear the music
Intense focus on her
She stands
Like a Greek statue
With a bounty of ripe fruit
On hip
The sweetest juice on Earth

Time stopped
My prey awaits
I will devour her
Make her part of me
Make me part of her
I send my malicious intent
Towards her

With a laser focused glance
She stares then looks away
I'm helpless—she isn't real
Like every dream I ever had
I don't want to wake up
I fight hard not to stare
Impossible thoughts
Deepest forces of nature
Are at work here
My fantasy reel spins out of control
The movie blazes through my eyes
I am the director
The producer
The leading man
She the lone actress
My focus locked and zooming
Extreme close-up
She glows
She wins all the awards
The air is electric

My groin is tight
I take off her cute overalls
Peeling them off slowly
Reality warped
It's almost real
I can feel her on me
Wrapped in my arms
Her skirt cut thigh high
Revealing her chiseled legs
Perfect vessels for transportation

She is of heaven
Soft-pale and tan
Sun-drenched lust
Evaporates me
Into a deeper dream
Her breasts are magic
Proud and firm
Nipples alert
Waiting to be exposed
My movie is swirling
The next scenes flash
I am behind her
I am full of love
Waiting to erupt
Movie stills flood past
Her youthful breasts
Fully Developed
Firmly in my grasp
Some women have tits
She has breasts
Like I said
She's a good girl
Fantasy in full swing
My screen is full
She melts the film
And sets the theater on fire
Her moan ramps up
To a pulsating scream
A siren only I can hear
Piercing
Through my ears

I thrust her torso forward
Grab her hips
She latches onto a pole
Hand over hand
Her patchwork overalls
Fall around her ankles
Lace panties pulled aside
A pink bow
For me to open
I thrust inside of her
Deep
Warm and hard
Savoring her pink flesh
Her pussy clenches and drips
Volcanic pain is swelling
My cock feels like steel
I'm strong
She wails
Her screams echo
Through the maze of tunnels
Red lights flashing
She surrenders
She is mine

Only for me

I stroke fast and hard
Slow and teasing
Her immature friend watches
She is homely
With small tits

I like small tits
She blushes
Continues to watch
Not blinking
Mouth agape
That's hot
The trolley is racing near
Bells ringing
I pump my hardest pumps
I'm gonna cum
Share my love in her.

Hold the Train!

Please don't cum yet
Just a few seconds away
Climax immanent
Rails screech
Trolley cars halt
To a dead stop
The doors open sideways
Reality pours out
Fantasy crashed
No survivors
My movie reel cuts
Theater turns black
No rolling credits
Mental recording taken
Archived in my vault
Home now
I close my eyes

I rewind the film
Play the movie again
In sweet
Super-slow motion
I jerk off
I cum fast
My hardest shot
My best performance
No acceptance speech
Needed.

Last Gasp

Death
A state
Sometimes a country
Out of this world
Non-existence
An unknown threshold
The greatest mystery
Of life
Unrevealed
Until the light is discovered
A journey begun
A journey's end
A life extinguished
Freedom from the corpse
Frightening first thought
An inevitable clock
In motion
Devastation
In final thought
Words never spoken
Truths never told

Words never spoken
The grave tells no secrets

Death can be

Long and brutal
Quick and merciful
Death triggers
Tragedy and sorrow
Suffering and pain
Tears and sobbing

Death relieves
Constraints of evil
An oppressor's final demise
Reprieve from their cruelty
Removed from your reality
Blindfold is off
Karmic justice
From death comes life
From life comes death
Unique
To each experience.

An Open Letter to Humanity

Are you happy now that the future has arrived? Is it as magical as you thought it would be? Everything that you hoped for and ever wanted. Robots to think and do everything for you? Everyone is afraid of big brother. Now you are one of his children by choice. You paid to have him in your pocket and hands. You can't see him but he can see you behind the screen you hide. A heavily filtered reality, posting and sharing only the pretty portraits of yourself. Encrypting the ugly ones behind a firewall to hide the truth, your truth. How others view you becomes your reality. A dirt cheap validation of likes and follows to soothe the insecurity and self-doubt of your fragile ego.

You have introduced your very own children to little brother and little sister. Making appointments for them to play with their friends indoors, safely tucked away with digital tags to see where their feet go.

Taking them to and from school in a helicopter. Lowering them cautiously into to their bubbles, cells without locks on either side of the door. Privacy is an ancient relic. Your thoughts and secrets are easily hacked, exposing you to a world that is desperate to know everything about everything, including you.

I look in the mirror, then out my window—always. The streets, parks, and backyards have been deserted, insular neighbors staying in their lanes as if traffic would cause an accident to their lives. May the two worlds never meet or mingle! May the pot stop melting together for the sake of progress!

In the future's future, there will be no need to speak, think, or write. Communication will be done by thinking alone, every thought and feeling broadcast into the ethos and beyond outer space, following it with giant telescopes to see where it goes, to find out who is listening light years away.

Then we all can say
Do you remember what is was like
Back then?

Hey, Little Man

I know you are scared
The attic door in your room
Has no monsters behind it
I know you are lonely
To the point of disappearing
The hole that you feel
Is the unknown
So many family secrets
Are being kept from you
This makes you sad and confused
In a house full of six children
Only you are missing a father
No one to show you
How to put the puzzle together
No dad to lack tracks
And send the train in motion
Ma loves the Father's Day cards
You make her in school
I know how shocking it was
When you asked her who 'he' was
She used the Santa Clause defense
"The Indians gave you to me."

She won't really give you back to them
When she is angry with you
The chief is not your father
You'll find out the truth one day
The familiar figure will surprise you
He has another family in town
You'll have a brother one day
You will travel and love
Fail and succeed
Your heart will break and heal
You will look for answers
In the bottom of a glass
You will find very few
I wish I could tell you
To put the glass down sooner
But you will
When you are ready
Hang in there, little man.
I will see you then.

Where Did You Go, Joe?

My best friend and brother
Joshua by name
He was always smiling
He was always depressed
With a tortured soul
He tried his best to be happy
He never was inside

He grew up on the beach
In a matchbox cottage
With too many kids
Somehow they fit
A plaque in his bathroom said

Friends are our chosen family
The truest thing I learned

We climbed Mt. Washington
With his dad and no map
We pushed and pulled

Each other up over every boulder
And up every steep cliff
Scary and exciting

I saved him from falling
The rocks crumbled under his feet
They dropped high and echoed below
We locked forearms and I pulled him up
His dad always thanked me for that

We drank hard and lived in the bars
Never picked up the hot girls
Always too shit-faced to score
One beyond drunk night
We threw paint filled beer bottles
Off the rusty water tower
Facing Boston Harbor
A red and white and blue masterpiece

The next morning the cops
Their signature house shaking knock
The sergeant showed us the paint trail
He scolded me and shook his head

JoJo had no brother
Neither did I
We never cried
Until I did

A bus load of sisters
Brothers bound by
Self-sabotage and failure
Addiction and circumstance
Similar and identical patterns
He had one child
Other than fathering her
He felt he failed in life
He returned home
To his childhood cottage
Sleeping in his childhood bed
Where we blared metal and rock cassettes
Blew cheap pot out the window
Dreamed of our future band
Stood on the roof and yelled at the moon

One blistering hot Friday night
After a long night
Of frying fish and sweating
At our old high school job
He took too many pills
He drank too much alcohol
He was tired and distant
His mother sent him to bed
With a cold drink in hand
He fell asleep sitting up

Having missed the
Saturday morning's breakfast
His mom and dad went to wake
Their beloved Joshua

For he had not come down
They went up
And he was motionless
Both windows wide open
Quiet and blue and at peace
Finally

The ocean waves went silent
The birds sang their saddest song
The air had escaped
The world began to deflate
Shaking in disbelief
His parents' hearts broke together
Their worst fears confirmed
For their beloved JoJo
Had not risen

At his wake the casket closed his face
His daughter drew in crayon
Loving and sorrow-filled notes

I love you, Daddy
I'll see you in heaven.

Pictures of father and daughter
Heart to heart
Arm in arm
Smile upon smile

At his funeral
They played *Beautiful Boy*
A soloist and a guitar
Strings that struck all chords
Tall and deep and far and wide
Pain and love resonated
The words wept quietly
I heard his voice in every lyric
His laugh in ever note
The mournful crowd
Cried and sang together

Near his grave stone
We wrote tiny notes
Of love and loss and hope
Tied them to colored balloons
Telling him we were sad
But it's OK
Loving tear smudged messages
To lift him high
Towards the heavenly gate

I haven't seen
Or talked to his family since
They were my family
And I was theirs
My heart is broken twice
My presence
Too harsh a reminder
Of their lost boy
I understand why

In his casket, I left a hand written note
Our favorite disc
Mad Season "Above"
Final goodbye
And an inside joke
JoJo my brother
I love you
I will always pray for you
My soul will never forget you
And my heart will always hear

Your song.

Blue Raven

(A song)

The ravens came and brought the winter rain
To witness me fading away
The battle wasn't right
The journey was all wrong
Shoulda been my last prayer
And my final song

The road I took was brutal at best
Midnight alleys, my friends laying dead
It should have been me
With the chalk around my head

My demons are fierce and the devil is strong

I was only awaken from the raven's caw
I told 'em my secrets—gave them my sins
Sent them with a message—begging once again
They returned with the news and sat on my grave
There was no one left, only myself to save

I survived all the crashes and near-death escapes
You had to look away, from the stain of my shame
I never blamed you, I woulda done the same
Being so close to heaven, I found myself inside
The only reason I'm alive, is because I could not die

Only God knows how many times I've tried
I drank up an ocean, a thousand miles wide
Stranded myself on an island
Way outta sight
You swam out so many times
And I threw your love away

When the ravens were gone, it melted my pain
My last prayer answered
Now God I believe in faith
I am here now, in the warm spring rain
Reaching for the sun
While the mud
Washes me away

Black-feathered angels
Saved me today.
Through the Lord's
Love

And shining grace.

IF YOU ARE HAVING THOUGHTS OF HARMING
YOURSELF OR ARE HAVING SUICIDAL
IDEATIONS

CALL 988
THE SUICIDE & CRISIS HOTLINE

SOMEONE WHO CARES IS THERE 24/7, TO LISTEN
TO YOU, AND HELP YOU IF YOU ARE WILLING TO
LET THEM. WHEN YOU HANG UP THE PHONE,
YOU ARE LEFT WITH A DECISION. YOU ARE
STILL IN DANGER FROM YOURSELF
IF YOU HAVE ACTIVE PLANS, OR ARE READY
AND PREPARED
TO TAKE YOUR OWN LIFE

CALL 911
IMMEDIATELY

YOU MUST BE REMOVED FROM THE
ENVIRONMENT WHERE YOU HAVE THE
MECHANICAL AND/OR CHEMICAL MEANS TO
KILL YOURSELF.
YOU HAVE A LIFE AND YOU ARE WORTH IT
IT DOES MATTER IF YOU ARE GONE
YOU ARE NOT ALONE
I SEE YOU
PLEASE CALL FOR HELP
I DID
AND IT SAVED MY LIFE

Printed in the USA
CPSIA information can be obtained
at www.ICGtesting.com
LVHW020809241023
761977LV00019B/54